J
595.76
Itel

DATE DUE

12-23-08			
APR 4 '09			
JUN 25 '09			
JAN 2 10			
FEB 18 10			
MAY 19 11			
JA 18 12			
JE 20 12			
MY 14 5			
GAYLORD			PRINTED IN U.S.A.

FIREFLIES

NICOLE HELGET

Published by Creative Education
P.O. Box 227, Mankato, Minnesota 56002
Creative Education is an imprint of The Creative Company

Design and production by Stephanie Blumenthal
Printed in the United States of America

Photographs by Alamy Images (blickwinkel, Phil Degginger), Getty Images
(Louise Tanguay, Photonica), J. E. Lloyd, University of Florida

Library of Congress Cataloging-in-Publication Data

Helget, Nicole Lea, 1976–
Fireflies / by Nicole Helget.
p. cm. — (BugBooks)
Includes index.
ISBN-13: 978-1-58341-542-9
1. Fireflies—Juvenile literature. I. Title.

QL596.L28H46 2007
595.76'44—DC22   2006018244

First Edition
2 4 6 8 9 7 5 3 1

THE MOON RISES ON A SUMMER NIGHT.

STARS SHINE IN THE SKY. LIGHT SPARKS FROM THE GRASS AND BETWEEN TREES. HAVE THE STARS FALLEN? NO. THE LIGHTS COME FROM FIREFLIES LIVING HERE ON EARTH!

FIREFLIES ARE INSECTS. THERE

ARE MORE THAN

2,000 KINDS OF

FIREFLIES. FIREFLIES

DO NOT LIVE VERY

LONG. SOME LIVE FOR

ONLY FIVE DAYS.

Most fireflies come out only at night.

FIREFLY FOOD Most adult fireflies do not eat anything. They live on the food they ate before they became adults. Adult fireflies just drink water. They drink **dew** right off of plants.

A FIREFLY HAS TWO EYES AND TWO FEELERS. THE EYES ARE VERY BIG. THEY CAN SEE IN MANY DIFFER- ENT DIRECTIONS.  THE FEELERS ARE CALLED ANTEN- NAE (AN-*TEN*-NAY). THEY HELP THE FIREFLY SMELL, FEEL, AND HEAR.

Fireflies use their eyes and feelers to explore.

A FIREFLY HAS SIX LEGS AND
FOUR WINGS. THE FRONT WINGS
PROTECT THE BACK
WINGS. THE BACK
WINGS ARE USED
FOR FLYING. FE-
MALE FIREFLIES DO
NOT FLY VERY MUCH. THEY LOOK
FOR PLACES TO LAY EGGS.

A firefly's long wings cover most of its body.

A FIREFLY'S LIGHT COMES FROM ITS BELLY. A FIREFLY HAS A LIGHT ORGAN THERE CALLED A LANTERN.

 IT IS YELLOW. FIRE-FLIES BLINK TO SEND MESSAGES TO EACH OTHER. THEN THE FE-MALE FIREFLIES LAY EGGS. A FIREFLY CAN LAY 100 EGGS.

A firefly's lantern is at the end of its belly.

A FIREFLY BEGINS LIFE AS A TINY

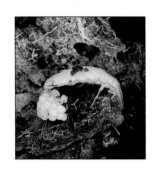 EGG THAT GLOWS. WHEN

THE EGG HATCHES, A

SMALL WORM COMES

OUT. THE WORM IS CALLED A "LARVA."

Firefly eggs glow. So do some firefly worms.

THE LARVA EATS LEAVES UNTIL ITS SKIN BECOMES TOO TIGHT. THE LARVA SHEDS ITS SKIN AND KEEPS GETTING BIGGER. WHEN THE LARVA IS BIG ENOUGH, IT RESTS. IT CHANGES INTO AN ADULT FIREFLY.

A larva grows wings and becomes an adult firefly.

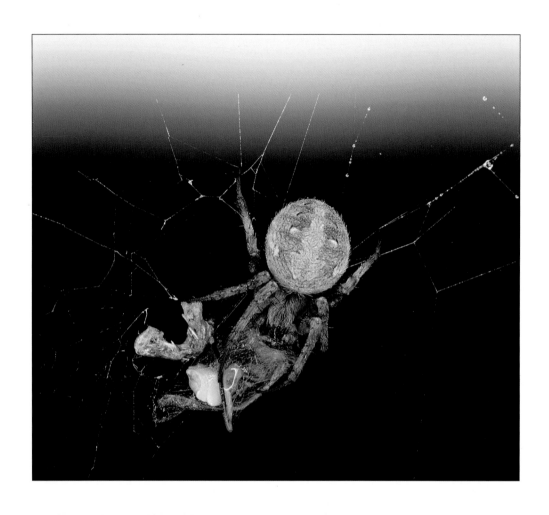

GLOWING FROGS Many animals like to eat fireflies. Fish and frogs like the taste of fireflies. Frogs that eat too many fireflies can glow!

FIREFLIES LIKE GRASSY AND WOODED AREAS THAT ARE DAMP.

THEY LIKE TO LIVE FAR FROM CITY LIGHTS. THE BRIGHTEST FIRE-FLIES LIVE IN TROPICAL AREAS. THESE ARE PLACES THAT ARE WARM AND OFTEN HAVE JUNGLES.

Fireflies have to watch out for hungry spiders.

FIREFLIES DON'T STING OR BURN PEOPLE. THEY ARE HELPFUL TO PEO-PLE.  FIREFLIES GAVE PEOPLE THE IDEA FOR FLASHLIGHTS. SCIEN-TISTS USE FIREFLIES TO MAKE NEW MEDICINES. SOME OF THESE MEDICINES HELP PEOPLE WHO HAVE CANCER.

Some people study fireflies up close.

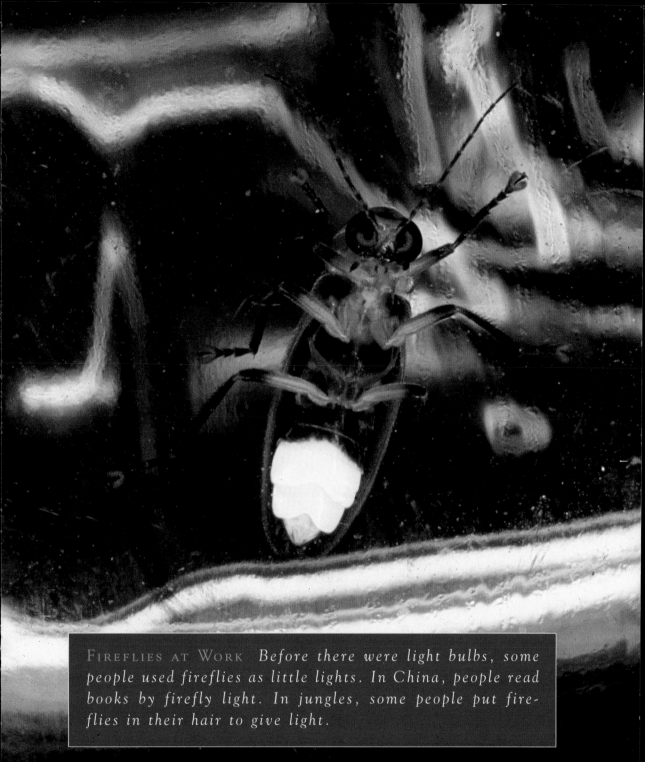

FIREFLIES AT WORK *Before there were light bulbs, some people used fireflies as little lights. In China, people read books by firefly light. In jungles, some people put fireflies in their hair to give light.*

COOL LIGHT *The light made by fireflies is not warm. If you catch a firefly, touch its belly. It will be cool. (After you catch fireflies, let them go!)*

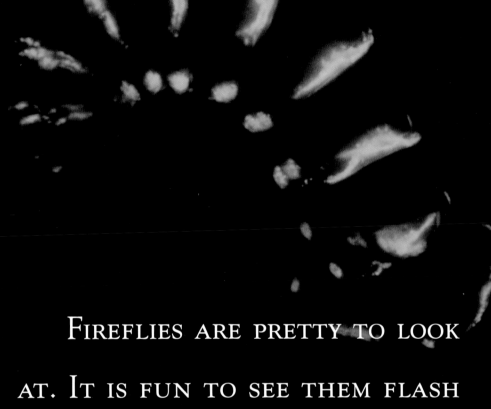

FIREFLIES ARE PRETTY TO LOOK
AT. IT IS FUN TO SEE THEM FLASH
ON AND OFF AT NIGHT. FIREFLIES
ARE LIKE LITTLE FLYING STARS!

Fireflies and glowing worms are fun to watch.

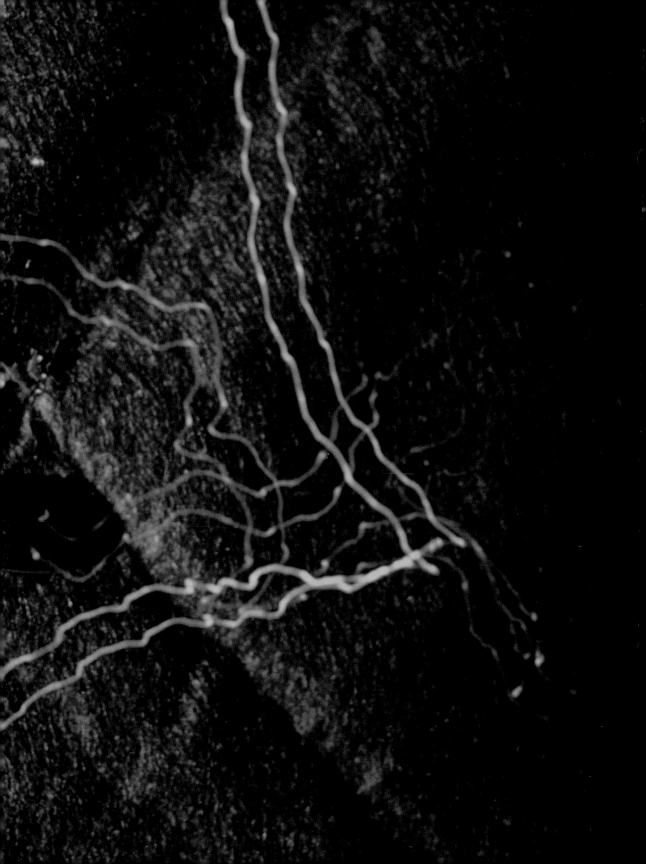

GLOSSARY

CANCER—A KIND OF SICKNESS THAT CAN MAKE PEOPLE DIE

DEW—DROPS OF WATER ON GRASS OR PLANTS

INSECTS—BUGS THAT HAVE SIX LEGS

ORGAN—A SPECIAL PART INSIDE THE BODY OF AN ANIMAL
OR PERSON

SHEDS—LOSES SKIN

INDEX

ANIMALS 16

ANTENNAE 7

EGGS 8, 11, 12

EYES 7

INSECTS 4, 23

LANTERN 11

LARVAE 12, 15

LEGS 8

LIFE SPAN 4

MEDICINES 18

SHEDDING 15, 23

WINGS 8